This Journal Belongs to:

La'Toya Guillory

ISBN:978-1-7348397-2-2

ENCOURAGEMENT FROM THE AUTHOR

This battle that you are fighting will require you to pick up your shield and fight. Remember that you fight not against flesh and blood, but against an enemy that's sole desire is to destroy everything that you have worked hard for. This will not be an easy fight, but if you allow God to go before you, He will give the enemy a fight he would have never imagined.

Peace I leave with you; my peace I give you. I do not give to you as the world gives. Do not let your hearts be troubled and do not be afraid. -John 14:27

_____

_____

_____

_____

_____

_____

_____

_____

_____

_____

_____

_____

_____

_____

_____

_____

_____

_____

_____

_____

_____

_____

_____

_____

_____

_____

_____

_____

_____

_____

_____

_____

_____

_____

_____

_____

_____

_____

_____

_____

_____

_____

_____

_____

_____

_____

_____

_____

House and wealth are inherited from fathers, but a prudent wife is from the Lord. -Proverbs 19:14

_____

_____

_____

_____

_____

_____

_____

_____

_____

_____

_____

_____

_____

_____

_____

_____

_____

_____

_____

_____

_____

_____

_____

_____

_____

_____

_____

_____

_____

_____

_____

Therefore, a man shall leave his father and his mother and hold fast to his wife, and they shall become one flesh.

-Genesis 2:24

_____

_____

_____

_____

_____

_____

_____

_____

_____

_____

_____

_____

_____

_____

_____

_____

_____

_____

_____

_____

_____

_____

_____

_____

_____

_____

_____

_____

_____

_____

_____

_____

_____

_____

_____

_____

_____

_____

_____

_____

_____

_____

_____

_____

_____

_____

_____

_____

_____

_____

_____

_____

Let marriage be held in honor among all, and let the marriage bed be undefiled, for God will judge the sexually immoral and adulterous.   *-Hebrews 13:4*

_____

_____

_____

_____

_____

_____

_____

_____

_____

_____

_____

_____

_____

_____

_____

_____

_____

_____

_____

_____

_____

_____

_____

_____

_____

_____

_____

_____

_____

_____

_____

_____

_____

And above all these put on love, which binds everything together in perfect harmony.   *-Colossians 3:14*

_____

_____

_____

_____

_____

_____

_____

_____

_____

_____

_____

_____

_____

_____

_____

_____

_____

_____

_____

_____

_____

_____

_____

_____

_____

_____

_____

_____

_____

_____

_____

_____

_____

_____

_____

_____

_____

_____

_____

_____

_____

_____

_____

_____

_____

_____

_____

_____

_____

_____

Likewise, husbands, live with your wives in an understanding way, showing honor to the woman as the weaker vessel, since they are heirs with you of the grace of life, so that your prayers may not be hindered. -1 Peter 3:7

_____

_____

_____

_____

_____

_____

_____

_____

_____

_____

_____

_____

_____

_____

_____

_____

_____

_____

_____

*So now faith, hope, and love abide, these three; but the
greatest of these is love.*   *-1 Corinthians 13:13*

_____

_____

_____

_____

_____

_____

_____

_____

_____

_____

_____

_____

_____

_____

_____

_____

_____

_____

_____

_____

_____

_____

_____

_____

_____

_____

_____

_____

_____

_____

_____

Husbands love your wives, as Christ loved the church and gave himself up for her.   *-Ephesians 5:25*

_____

_____

_____

_____

_____

_____

_____

_____

_____

_____

_____

_____

_____

_____

_____

_____

_____

_____

_____

_____

_____

_____

_____

_____

_____

_____

_____

_____

_____

_____

However, let each one of you love his wife as himself, and let the wife see that she respects her husband.

-Ephesians 5: 33

_____

_____

_____

_____

_____

_____

_____

_____

_____

_____

_____

_____

_____

_____

_____

_____

_____

_____

_____

_____

_____

_____

_____

_____

_____

_____

_____

_____

_____

_____

_____

_____

_____

UNSHAKEABLE MARRIAGE JOURNAL

Above all, keep loving one another earnestly, since love covers a multitude of sins.   *-1 Peter 4:8*

_____

_____

_____

_____

_____

_____

_____

_____

_____

_____

_____

_____

_____

_____

_____

_____

_____

_____

And though a man might prevail against one who is alone, two will withstand him—a threefold cord is not quickly broken.   *-Ecclesiastes 4:12*

_____

_____

_____

_____

_____

_____

_____

_____

_____

_____

_____

_____

_____

_____

_____

_____

_____

_____

_____

_____

_____

_____

_____

_____

_____

_____

_____

_____

_____

An excellent wife is the crown of her husband, but she who brings shame is like rottenness in his bones. -Proverbs 12:4

_____

_____

_____

_____

_____

_____

_____

_____

_____

_____

_____

_____

_____

_____

_____

_____

_____

_____

_____

_____

_____

_____

_____

_____

_____

_____

_____

_____

_____

_____

_____

_____

_____

_____

_____

_____

_____

_____

_____

_____

_____

_____

_____

_____

_____

_____

_____

_____

_____

_____

_____

And we know that in all things God works for the good of those who love him, who have been called according to his purpose. -*Romans 8:28*

_____

_____

_____

_____

_____

_____

_____

_____

_____

_____

_____

_____

_____

Be on your guard; stand firm in the faith; be courageous; be strong.   -1 Corinthians 16:13

_____

_____

_____

_____

_____

_____

_____

_____

_____

_____

_____

_____

_____

_____

_____

_____

_____

_____

_____

_____

_____

_____

_____

_____

_____

_____

_____

_____

_____

_____

_____

_____

_____

_____

_____

_____

_____

_____

_____

_____

_____

_____

_____

_____

_____

_____

Two are better than one, because they have a good reward for their toil. For if they fall, one will lift up his fellow. But woe to him who is alone when he falls and has not another to lift him up! Again, if two lie together, they keep warm, but how can one keep warm alone? And though a man might prevail against one who is alone, two will withstand him-a threefold cord is not easily broken.

-Ecclesiastes 4:9-12

_____

_____

_____

_____

_____

_____

_____

_____

_____

_____

_____

_____

_____

_____

_____

_____

_____

_____

_____

_____

_____

_____

_____

_____

_____

_____

_____

_____

_____

_____

_____

_____

What therefore God has joined together, let not man separate.   *-Mark 10:9*

_____

_____

_____

_____

_____

_____

_____

_____

_____

_____

_____

_____

_____

_____

_____

Steadfast love and faithfulness meet; righteousness and peace kiss each other.   *-Psalm 85:10*

_____

_____

_____

_____

_____

_____

_____

_____

_____

_____

_____

_____

_____

_____

_____

_____
_____
_____
_____
_____
_____
_____
_____
_____
_____
_____
_____
_____
_____
_____
_____
_____

_____

_____

_____

_____

_____

_____

_____

_____

_____

_____

_____

_____

_____

_____

_____

_____

_____

_____

so is my word that goes out from my mouth: It will not return to me empty but will accomplish what I desire and achieve the purpose for which I sent it.   *-Isaiah 55:11*

_____

_____

_____

_____

_____

_____

_____

_____

_____

_____

_____

_____

_____

_____

_____

_____

_____

_____

_____

_____

_____

_____

_____

_____

_____

_____

_____

_____

_____

_____

God is not human, that he should lie, not a human being, that he should change his mind. Does he speak and then not act? Does he promise and not fulfill? -Numbers 23:19

_____

_____

_____

_____

_____

_____

_____

_____

_____

_____

_____

_____

_____

_____

_____

_____

_____

_____

_____

_____

_____

_____

_____

_____

_____

_____

_____

_____

_____

_____

_____

_____

_____

For as a young man marries a young woman, so shall your sons marry you, and as the bridegroom rejoices over the bride, so shall your God rejoice over you. -Isaiah 62:5

_____

_____

_____

_____

_____

_____

_____

_____

_____

_____

_____

_____

_____

_____

_____

_____

_____

_____

_____

_____

_____

_____

_____

_____

_____

_____

_____

_____

_____

Love is patient and kind; love does not envy or boast; it is not arrogant or rude. It does not insist on its own way; it is not irritable or resentful; it does not rejoice at wrongdoing but rejoices with the truth. Love bears all things, believes all things, hopes all things, endures all things. Love never ends. As for prophecies, they will pass away; as for tongues, they will cease; as for knowledge, it will pass away.   *-1 Corinthians 13:4-8*

_____

_____

_____

_____

_____

_____

_____

_____

_____

_____

_____

_____

_____

A new commandment I give to you, that you love one another: just as I have loved you, you also are to love one another. By this all people will know that you are my disciples, if you have love for one another."

-John 13:34-35

Let all that you do be done in love. -1 Corinthians 16:14

_____

_____

_____

_____

_____

_____

_____

_____

_____

_____

_____

_____

_____

_____

_____

It is better to live in a corner of the housetop than in a house shared with a quarrelsome wife.   -Proverbs 21:9

_____

_____

_____

_____

_____

_____

_____

_____

_____

_____

_____

_____

_____

_____

_____

Beloved, let us love one another, for love is from God, and whoever loves has been born of God and knows God. Anyone who does not love does not know God, because God is love.   *-1 John 4:7-8*

La'Toya Guillory is new to the writing scene. She was born in Atlantic City, New Jersey in 1981, but has been a native of Lafayette, Louisiana for the last 21 years. For years, La'Toya has worked in the social service field and has seen the effects of individuals who live life as if they have no purpose. Her writing style is one that strives to empower individuals to live according to the purpose that God has for them. La'Toya is the owner of Empowered with Purpose LLC which serves as the catalyst to empower her community. She is the author of her first book, Anchored: Anchored in Christ, Anchored in Marriage. She was recently awarded Acadiana's Top 20 Leaders under 40 in 2018. She is a certified marriage enrichment facilitator for Prepare and Enrich and SYMBIS (Saving Your Marriage Before it Starts). She graduated with her bachelor's degree in Child and Family Studies in 2006 and went on to complete her master's degree in Human Services Counseling with Specialization in Marriage and Families, in 2017.

" My hope, is that you come to the realization that you have a purpose and God wants to use you for such a time as this."
-La'Toya Guillory-

AVAILABLE NOW!!!!

VISIT HTTPS://EMPOWEREDWITHPURPOSE.NET

Made in the USA
Columbia, SC
19 November 2023

26468036R00085